W9-AMW-728

ideals®
CHRISTMAS

The greatest Christmas gift of all
Was never placed beneath a tree,
But lay within a manger bed,
Beneath a star, for all to see.

Emily Scarlett

ISBN 0-8249-1056-7

Publisher, Patricia A. Pingry
Editor, Peggy Schaefer
Art Director, Lyman Black, Jr.
Production Manager, Jan Johnson
Permissions, Kathleen Gilbert

IDEALS—Vol. 44, No. 8 December MCMLXXXVII IDEALS (ISSN 0019-137X) is published eight times a year,
February, March, May, June, August, September, November, December
by IDEALS PUBLISHING CORPORATION, Nelson Place at Elm Hill Pike, Nashville, Tenn. 37214-8000
Second class postage paid at Nashville, Tennessee, and additional mailing offices.
Copyright © MCMLXXXVII by IDEALS PUBLISHING CORPORATION
POSTMASTER: Send address changes to Ideals, Post Office Box 148000, Nashville, Tenn. 37214-8000
All rights reserved. Title IDEALS registered U.S. Patent Office.
Published simultaneously in Canada.

SINGLE ISSUE—$3.95
ONE-YEAR SUBSCRIPTION—eight consecutive issues as published—$15.95
TWO-YEAR SUBSCRIPTION—sixteen consecutive issues as published—$27.95
Outside U.S.A., add $4.00 per subscription year for postage and handling.

Front and back covers by Fred Sieb

Inside front cover by Bob Taylor
Inside back cover from Freelance Photographers Guild

December

December is the magic month
Of all the whole long year;
Despite the cold, it holds a warmth,
A world of Christmas cheer.
We welcome this so happy month,
The beauty of the snow,
And feel the miracle of love
Within the candleglow.

December is a month of dreams
When little hearts are gay;
And children talk of Santa Claus,
Enjoying hours of play.
The woods are silent in the dawn,
A quiet over all;
But firesides glow with happiness
Beside the tree so tall.

It's time for gifts and treasured cards,
For mistletoe and holly,
A star so bright atop the tree,
Old Santa Claus so jolly.
When hearts know tender love and peace,
Each joy we still remember;
No other month in all the year
Is lovely as December.

Garnett Ann Schultz

Photo Opposite
CONWAY, NEW HAMPSHIRE
Fred Sieb

Photo Overleaf
STEAMBOAT, COLORADO
Gregory Edwards
International Stock Photo

Christmas Tea Cozy

*To make the tea cozy pictured on
the opposite page, follow the instructions below.*

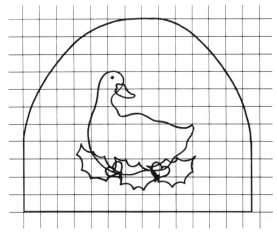

TEA COZY PATTERN
each square equals one inch

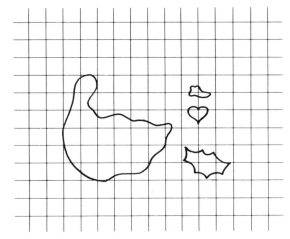

APPLIQUE PATTERNS
each square equals one inch

Materials Needed:
- ⅔ **yard tartan cotton fabric**
- ⅔ **yard bonded polyester batting**
- ¾ **yard pre-gathered, 2-inch-wide white lace**
- ¼ **yard red satin ribbon, ⅜-inch wide**
- **Green, red, white, and tan cotton broadcloth scraps**
- **Thread to match fabrics used**

Construction:

STEP 1 - Cutting cozy pieces

Fold fabric in half, with selvages together. Fold in half again, selvages to center fold.

Pin cozy pattern to fabric, aligning bottom edge of pattern piece with selvages and center fold. Cut. Cut through center fold. You should now have four identical pieces cut from fabric.

Using same pattern piece, cut two pieces from polyester batting for tea cozy stuffing.

STEP 2 - Preparing appliqués

Press interfacing to broadcloth pieces.

Pin appliqué pattern pieces to fabric and cut shapes: 1 duck; 1 duck bill; 2 hearts; and 3 pieces of holly.

STEP 3 - Attaching lace

With right sides together, pin lace to one of the cozy pieces which has been placed on one of the pieces of batting. Baste along the curved edge, leaving a ½-inch seam allowance.

STEP 4 - Attaching appliqué

Pin duck shape to cozy front (the form to which lace has been basted). Sew along outer edge of duck, using a medium zig-zag stitch. (Matching thread is recommended. A fine stitch length works best.)

Repeat this process for remaining appliqué pieces.

Use a zig-zag stitch to sew in duck's eye.

STEP 5 - Attaching front to back

With right sides together, place cozy back on front. Place remaining piece of batting on top of cozy back. Pin all four layers together.

Stitch through all layers along the basted lace seam line. Clip curves.

Press seams open at bottom edge.

STEP 6 - Attaching lining to cozy

With right sides together, stitch remaining cozy pieces together, leaving a ½-inch seam allowance.

Press the seams of the lining open at bottom edge.

With right sides together, pin bottom edges of lining and cozy together. Leaving a 5-inch opening along cozy back, stitch the pieces together, using a ½-inch seam allowance.

Pull the cozy and lining through the opening. Press lightly.

Tuck the lining into the cozy. Hand-sew the opening on the tea cozy back.

STEP 7 - Finishing the cozy

Tack top of lining to inside top of cozy to hold in place.

Make a bow from satin ribbon. Hand-sew to appliquéd duck.

Ann Marie Braaten

Photo Opposite
TEA TIME
Steve Jackson

Table setting courtesy of Tabletop & Gifts, Nashville, Tennessee

The season's first snowflakes
   flirt with my wipers.
December.
   Already.

"Impossible!"
   I say aloud
to a passing semi piled high
   with a load of Christmas trees,
      their scented boughs
      bound with brown twine.

The mall now boasts
   a festive look—
white lights wink
   through wisps of
      plastic greenery,
poinsettias pose
   behind plate glass,
giant candy canes
   stand sentry
      inside display windows.

The twang of
   worn Christmas records
      ripples from square black speakers.

Santa sits in a
   scarlet sleigh;
his eyes look tired.
A petite blond in
   skimpy red velvet
      snaps picture
         after
         picture.

I haven't begun

to think yet of
   Christmas, God.

My refrigerator
is still filled with
   leftover turkey,
   dried-out dressing.

Yet Christmas is here,
   its presence as tangible as
      cardboard snowflakes
         suspended on silver threads
         high above my head.

Help me this year, Lord,
   to sidestep the surge of
      commercialism,
      materialism
that swirls around me
   in colorful waves.

Above the BRRINGG of cash registers,
   the ripping of Christmas wrap
let me hear the
   rustle of swaddling cloth
      cradled in straw.

In the midst of
   bow-making,
      cookie-baking,
let me take time for
   the most important
      preparation
of all—

   the opening of
   my own heart
      to you.

Mary Lou Carney

Christmas Cards

How lovely are the sentiments
    Contained in Christmas cards,
As well as dear heartwarming scenes
    Of snowy trees and yards!
They never change so very much—
    But who would want it so?
For Christmas seems to always belong
    To cedar trees and snow.

The greetings on a Christmas card
    Are precious as a gem,
Because old neighbors and old friends
    Send us their love with them—
Warming our hearts with loving words,
    Making us know that they
Are thinking of our bygone times
    Upon this Christmas Day.

A holly wreath, a little church,
    A lovely lighted door,
Some carol singers in the street,
    The windows of a store—
All these are part of Christmastime,
    Like cake and mistletoe,
Because a card arrived today
    And joyfully said so.

Edna Jaques

Photo Opposite
CHRISTMAS WORDS
H. Armstrong Roberts

Winter

I like to walk in winter's
  snow,
To hear the gusty north wind
  blow
And feel its icy fingers on
  my cheek.

I like to hear the children
  shout
As happily they play about
And watch the skaters
  gliding on the creek.

It is again that time of year
For jolly snowmen to appear
To cheer the young, as well
  as young at heart.

And when the moon is all
  aglow,
It places diamonds on the
  snow
And snowflakes dance to set
  the time apart.

Muriel E. Glenn
Cambridge Springs, PA

Just for Children?

Is Christmas just for children,
Just for youngsters to enjoy?
Don't leave your childhood
  behind
Like some discarded toy.

Think back to all the magic
In a late December snow,
And see the brilliant sparkle
Of the moonlight's steady
  glow.

Christmas hymns and loving
  friends,
The lighting of the tree,
Presents picked with
  thoughtfulness
And hidden carefully,

Gingerbread and pumpkin
  pies,
A turkey roasting slow,
All these are part of
  Christmas Day
And ever will be so.

The story of the Christ Child
And the things we've held
  so dear
Should not be dimmed by
  age or time;
They're born anew each year.

Gail Payne
Yelm, WA

Reflections

Christmas

Christmas comes but once
    every year,
Bringing glad tidings, and
    lots of good cheer,
Telling to all, that our Savior
    was born
On a calm, cold, December
    morn.
In a manger, on a bed of hay,
Wrapped in swaddling
    clothes, he lay.
"No room at the inn," was
    what one had said,
So in a stable Mary made
    his bed.
Let us remember that
    Christmas morn,
When Our Lord Jesus was
    really born.

Frances Symoniak
Greendale, WI

Fragrance of Christmas

The fragrance of Christmas
Kindles memories divine
Of spicy fresh gingerbread
Mingled with pine;
Of bayberry candles softly
    aglow;
Of peppermint, chocolate,
The freshness of snow.
Tender cookies, sweet and
    warm,
Mince pie and plum pudding
All add to the charm.
Consult not the calendar,
December comes round
When the fragrance of
    Christmas
In each home abounds.

Nancy L. Kratowicz
Port Richey, FL

Editor's Note: Readers are invited to submit unpublished, original poetry, short anecdotes, and humorous reflections on life for possible publication in future *Ideals* issues. Please send copies only; manuscripts will not be returned. Writers will receive $10 for each published submission. Send materials to "Readers' Reflections," Ideals Publishing Corporation, Nelson Place at Elm Hill Pike, Nashville, Tennessee 37214.

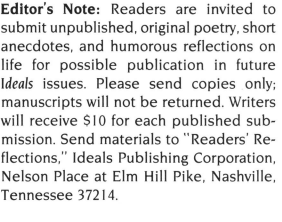

The Heart Takes Wing at Christmastime

The heart takes flight at
  Christmastime
And somehow wends its way
Through the snow and sleet and
  storms of life
To home of yesterday.

For there a certain charm
  surrounds
That home, wherever it be—
On mountain high, in valley low,
Or by the shining sea.

The heart takes wing at
  Christmastime
And finds its way back home
To memory-laden, pleasant rooms
Where seeds of love were sown.

It's true, the year is filled with
  cares
But naught can draw the line
To keep the heart from going home
Come joyful Christmastime.

Loise Pinkerton Fritz

Painting Opposite
EVENTIDE
John Slobodnik

The Most Merry Christmas Tree

Our Christmas tree is crooked;
Some lights are burnt out, too.
Our homemade decorations
Only cost a cent or two.

But there is something special
About our simple tree—
The little boys who trimmed it
Mean so very much to me.

Every piece was chosen
And handled with great care.
The bread dough star hung here,
The paper manger there,

Ornaments which once were gifts,
Homemade paper chains,
Plastic bells and satin balls,
And scrumptious candy canes.

Our tree may not be fancy
(There's one old patchwork mouse),
But one thing we have plenty of
Is love within this house.

An angel atop the tree
Reminds us of the boy
Whose one life touched the world
To bring us love and joy.

Early Christmas morning,
Gifts of love we bring
To celebrate the birthday
Of Jesus Christ our King.

The spirit that surrounds it,
I'm sure you will agree,
Makes ours a very special
And most merry Christmas tree.

Yvonne Patterson

Painting Opposite
CHRISTMAS TREE MERRIMENT
M.K. Edwards

Christmas Duties

Hang up the holly, the wreath of good cheer!
This time is so jolly, the best of the year.
Tack up the mistletoe, the sweetheart's delight;
Let it swing to and fro over hearts gay and light.

Dress up the fir tree! Hang tinsel bright
For that jolly old visitor on Christmas night.
Hang up the stockings all in a row
For Sister and Brother who love Christmas so.

Light up the Yule log! Let each cheery spark
Shine down in your heart and chase out the dark.
Pull out that smile you've been hiding all year.
Greet all with "Merry Christmas!" and lots of good cheer.

Zenith Hess

Hanging Decorations

Mother hung the holly wreath
Upon the wide front door;
Jimmy hung the silvery bells
On the Christmas tree once more.

Susie hung the dazzling balls
On the pine tree row by row;
Daddy winked at Mommy
As he hung the mistletoe!

Lovely cards hung here and there
From friends both far and near;
Isn't it strange how hanging things
Can add to Christmas cheer?

Ruth H. Underhill

CHRISTMAS SLED

I remember the thrill of riding downhill
    With everyone laughing and gay,
A gang on the sled and the moon overhead
    And the hillside lighter than day.

It held quite a few, so girls and boys, too,
    Piled on with a shout of delight;
The one on the end would have to attend
    To the push that got us off right,

And then in a flash jump on with a dash
    Or the bobsled would leave him behind.
The air was too cold and the wind rather bold,
    But never did anyone mind;

With seldom a spill we sped down the hill
    Taking the chill spray in stride.
Over rock-hard snow with faces aglow—
    Always a heart-stopping ride!—

Our steel-runnered steed would gather up speed
    To swoop past small sleds on each side.
Over the tracks with the wind at our backs
    We'd fly and then drift to a stop;

Then back up the hill we'd trudge with a will,
    Careful to keep to the side.
All hands on the rope, we'd pull up the slope
    For one more breathtaking ride.

Harriet Whipple

The Magic of Christmas

There's a glowing kind of magic
When Christmastime draws near.
You can see it all around you
Bringing special joy and cheer.

The children's smiling faces
All hold wonder and delight
And always perfect faith
That Santa will make his flight.

Shoppers hurry to and fro
Along the avenue,
Laughing as they move along
With presents bright and new.

Crystal snowflakes dance and swirl
In merry downward flight;
Street and field and rooftop
Lie under a blanket of white.

The candle stars in heaven
Shine radiant above,
While Christmas bells ring out
A song of peace and love.

Christmas trees are all bedecked,
And mistletoe and holly
Hang in rich abundance
To make this season jolly.

Christmastime for young and old
Is filled with magic glow,
As all rejoice the birth
Of the Christ Child long ago.

LaVerne P. Larson

The Candy Cane

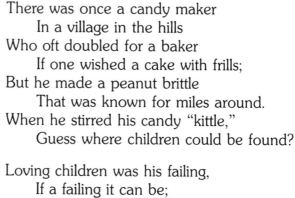

There was once a candy maker
    In a village in the hills
Who oft doubled for a baker
    If one wished a cake with frills;
But he made a peanut brittle
    That was known for miles around.
When he stirred his candy "kittle,"
    Guess where children could be found?

Loving children was his failing,
    If a failing it can be;
And a group was always trailing
    For the "tastes" that would be free.
How he ever made a living
    Those who knew him couldn't say
For they always saw him giving
    All his precious wares away.

Just before one Christmas season
    Early mornings he'd arise
Cause he had this special reason:
    He so wanted to surprise
All the tots with a confection
    In a brand new Christmas mold;
But with all his deep reflection
    No new pattern would unfold.

Then one dawn this would-be treater
    Had his eyes squeezed to a squint.
Lo! He'd left too near the heater
    All his sticks of peppermint.
There like shepherd crooks they rested!
    The old man could scarce believe
That he had what he'd requested
    For the tots on Christmas Eve.

Margaret Rorke

Santa Passes

Edgar A. Guest

I don't know as I was entirely happy that last Christmas. We have had Santa Claus with us as a real and genuine saint all down through the years, but I suspect that he has come to us now for the last time.

It happens to every family, I supppose. Christmas from now on, of course, will be as happy as possible, but it will be different. By the time the boy was ready to say good-bye to Santa, little Janet was ready to welcome him, and so we carried on. There is no baby in our house now, and when Janet dismisses him, the jolly old fellow will have to look elsewhere for welcome. I shall miss him, I think, because his visits have meant so much fun. I have enjoyed telling about him as much as Janet has enjoyed hearing about him. He has been a part of our family life. His comings have been looked forward to and planned for.

But this year I have noticed that upon that little mind has fallen the seed of doubt. Those eyes of hers have learned a subtle wink. I think she and her brother have a secret confidence. Wisdom has begun its work. She has begun to mistrust where once she wholeheartedly believed, and I am sorry that it is so. From now on, only the deadly, dull, dry fact will be hers. The delights of elusion and fancy will be no more.

This is called growing old. I am sure she is giving up Santa Claus, but I hope that to the end of her life she will retain the love that made his visits possible.

Well, it was a Merry Christmas, of that fact
    there is no doubt;
The little house proclaims it, for the toys are
    strewn about.
From the break of day till bedtime there was
    laughter in the place,
But I fancied that I noticed something curious
    in her face.
In the midst of the excitement there would
    come a wistful pause,
And I somehow have the notion that's the last
    of Santa Claus.
Down the years we've had him with us; every
    Merry Christmas Day
Santa Claus has paid his visit in the good old-
    fashioned way.
For when Buddy rose to boyhood, little Janet
    came along,

But I somehow have the notion she suspects
    there's something wrong;
For I thought that I detected in her conduct,
    now and then,
A break in her devotion to the jolliest of men.

She hung her little stocking by the fireplace as
    of old,
And she gave a cheer for Santa, but it lacked
    the ring of gold,
And though Christmas Day was merry, I
    began to realize
That our lovely little baby now is growing very
    wise;
And I can't help feeling saddened and
    regretful, just because
I am sure our house last Christmas saw the
    end of Santa Claus.

Painting Overleaf
George Hinke

Home for Christmas

Editor's Note for "Home for Christmas"

In 1881, two months before her sixteenth birthday, Laura Ingalls Wilder was hired to teach a winter school term in an abandoned claim shanty twelve miles from DeSmet, Dakota Territory where her family was living.

The school was drafty and cold, and Laura's living conditions were miserable. She was painfully homesick for Pa and Ma and Carrie and Grace, who were wintering comfortably in Pa's store building in DeSmet.

To spare her from homesick weekends, young homesteader Almanzo Wilder regularly drove out from town to squire Laura home. She expected her rides behind Almanzo's Morgans to end when her first school term ended; however, he came courting for three years and continued to appear at Laura's schools until she agreed to marry him.

At Christmastime in 1924, more than forty years after Almanzo's fearless drives over the bitter-cold prairies, Laura warmly recalled the "man of the place" and his dashing team saving her from a miserable Christmas miles away from home. She shared this story with her *Missouri Ruralist* readers, noting that at Christmastime "our hearts grow tender with childhood memories."

William Anderson

The snow was scudding low over the drifts of the white world outside the little claim shanty. It was blowing through the cracks in its walls and forming little piles and miniature drifts on the floor and even on the desks before which several children sat, trying to study; for this abandoned claim shanty that had served as the summer home of a homesteader on the Dakota prairies was being used as a schoolhouse during the winter.

The walls were made of one thickness of wide boards with cracks between, and the enormous stove that stood nearly in the center of the one room could scarcely keep out the frost though its sides were a glowing red. The children were dressed warmly and had been allowed to gather closely around the stove, following the advice of the county superintendent of schools, who on a recent visit had said that the only thing he had to say to them was to keep their feet warm.

This was my first school, I'll not say how many years ago, but I was only sixteen years old and twelve miles from home during a frontier winter. I walked a mile over the unbroken snow from my boarding place to school every morning and back at night. There were only a few pupils and on this particular snowy afternoon they were restless, for it was nearing four o'clock and tomorrow was Christmas. "Teacher" was restless, too, though she tried not to show it, for she was wondering if she could get home for Christmas Day.

It was almost too cold to hope for Father to

come, and a storm was hanging in the northwest which might mean a blizzard at any minute. Still, tomorrow was Christmas—and then there was a jingle of sleigh bells outside. A man in a huge fur coat in a sleigh full of robes passed the window. I was going home after all!

When one thinks of twelve miles now, it is in terms of motor cars and means only a few minutes. It was different then, and I'll never forget that ride. The bells made a merry jingle and the fur robes were warm, but the weather was growing colder and the snow was drifting, so that the horses must break their way through the drifts.

We were facing the strong wind and every little while he, who later became the "man of the place," must stop the team, get out in the snow, and by putting his hands over each horse's nose in turn, thaw the ice from them where the breath had frozen over their nostrils. Then he would get back into the sleigh and on we'd go until once more the horses could not breathe for the ice.

When we reached the journey's end, it was forty degrees below zero, the snow was blowing so thickly that we could not see across the street, and I was so chilled that I had to be half carried into the house. But I was home for Christmas and cold and danger were forgotten.

Such magic there is in Christmas to draw the absent ones home, and if unable to go in the body, the thoughts will hover there! Our hearts grow tender with childhood memories and love of kindred, and we are better throughout the year for having in spirit become a child again at Christmastime.

Laura Ingalls Wilder

Magnificat

And he shall suckle at my breast,
And lie upon my knee;
And he shall say his childhood prayer
And cuddle close to me;
And I shall tell him bible tales
Seated upon the sod;
Ah, wonder, that my baby boy
Should be the Son of God!

Of me, the maid of low estate,
Messiah must be born,
And yet men gaze with ribald mirth
And evil eyes of scorn.
The kindly neighbors draw apart
To whisper words of blame,
And patient Joseph, sad at heart,
Must share with me my shame.

Ah, woe is me, and mine the woe!
For he, my babe unborn
Must grow to be a man of grief,
Afflicted and forlorn.
Blessed above all humankind
In all the world am I,
Yet I must stand at Calvary
And watch my baby die.

Yet he shall sit on David's throne,
Inviolate of old;
And he shall be the promised seed
Of whom the prophet told.
My soul doth magnify the Lord,
My heart doth sing for joy;
Oh, wonder, that the Son of God
Should be my baby boy.

Frederick H. Sterne

Painting Opposite
MOTHER AND CHILD
Sandro Botticelli
The Louvre, Paris, France
(Photo, The Photo Source)

Through the Eyes of a Child

During one Advent, a wee child of three,
Crayon in hand, drew the Christ Child for me.
Touched by her picture, I pulled the girl near
And asked her of details that I thought unclear.

"Each star has two dots—why is it that way?"
She answered, "They're eyes—to look down where He lay."
"Why from a cow's mouth did you draw that smoke flowing?"
She answered, "It's not smoke—the cattle are lowing."

"I see you drew wisemen—five and not three."
Her eyes gleamed with brightness: "That's you and that's me!"
Through crayon and paper the Christ Child can come
In love gifts of wisdom from those who are young.

O Father, please grant old adult folks like me
The blessing to see Christ through eyes that are three.

Debbie W. Parvin

Painting Overleaf
NATIVITY SCENE
Frances Hook

The Christmas Story

And the angel said unto her, Fear not, Mary: for thou hast found favour with God.

And, behold, thou shalt conceive in thy womb, and bring forth a son, and shalt call his name Jesus.

He shall be great, and shall be called the Son of the Highest: and the Lord God shall give unto him the throne of his father David:

And he shall reign over the house of Jacob for ever; and of his kingdom there shall be no end.

Luke 1:30-33

And she brought forth her firstborn son, and wrapped him in swaddling clothes, and laid him in a manger; because there was no room for them in the inn.

And there were in the same country shepherds abiding in the field, keeping watch over their flock by night.

And, lo, the angel of the Lord came upon them, and the glory of the Lord shone round about them: and they were sore afraid.

And the angel said unto them, Fear not: for, behold, I bring you good tidings of great joy, which shall be to all people.

For unto you is born this day in the city of David a Saviour, which is Christ the Lord.

Luke 2:7-11

Then Herod, when he had privily called the wise men, inquired of them diligently what time the star appeared.

And he sent them to Bethlehem, and said, Go and search diligently for the young child; and when ye have found him, bring me word again, that I may come and worship him also.

When they had heard the king, they departed; and, lo, the star which they saw in the east, went before them, till it came and stood over where the young child was.

When they saw the star, they rejoiced with exceeding great joy.

And when they were come into the house, they saw the young child with Mary his mother, and fell down, and worshipped him: and when they had opened their treasures, they presented unto him gifts; gold, and frankincense, and myrrh.

And being warned of God in a dream that they should not return to Herod, they departed into their own country another way.

Matthew 2:7-12

There is nothing I can give you which you have not; but there is much that, while I cannot give, you can take. No heaven can come to us unless our hearts find rest in it today. ····· Take heaven. No peace lies in the future which is not hidden in this present instant. Take peace. The gloom of the world is but a shadow; behind it, yet within reach, is joy. Take joy. And so, at this Christmastime, I greet you with the prayer that for you, now and forever, the daybreak and the shadows flee away. ·:·~·:·

Fra Giovanni

The Second Christmas

Mary looked up from the muddy water at the river's edge and watched, smiling, as her young son struggled to keep his balance. His chubby legs wobbled and his dimpled arms beat at the air as he strained to take each step. She laughed aloud as the little boy finally lost his balance and plopped down on the dusty path. For a moment he looked as though he might cry, but then a bright orange poppy caught his eye. He crawled over to examine it more closely.

Mary turned back to her washing, dunking and squeezing it rhythmically in the flowing stream. Soon Jesus toddled back to the water and sat down awkwardly next to her.

"And what are you about today, my little one?" Mary asked the wide-eyed child. Giggling in reply, he splashed his bare toes in the lapping water and tossed handfuls of sand into the air.

Mary wrung out the clothes and tossed them into a basket, then sat down to rest for a moment beside the stream. She studied her son as he played, his dark curls bouncing with each movement.

Tomorrow her little Jesus would be a year old. How different, she thought, this year would be from the last. Since then the little family of three had fled from their homeland into the unfamiliarity of Egypt. Mary wondered how long their stay would be. She yearned for the faces of her family. She longed to show them her firstborn son, to hear them praise his beauty and his infant accomplishments. She sighed, lost in her thoughts.

Sensing his mother's unrest, the little boy nestled against her. Pulling himself up by her sleeve, he placed a grubby hand against his mother's cheek. Instinctively, Mary took the child in her arms, loosened her garment, and began to nurse him. As he settled against her, she hummed a quiet lullaby.

Her mind still had trouble reconciling all the contradictions of this little one. He was the Son of God, yet he depended on her for life. He was a miracle, yet so like any other child. He looked as others did, but he carried the beauty of holiness within him. How could this little hand, now so tightly curled around her fingers, have formed mankind? She studied the tiny lips that could not yet speak a word. How could they have ordered the universe into being, separated light from darkness and sea from land?

Satisfied, the child wriggled around in his mother's lap and babbled in contentment. Mary began to sing the song placed in her heart when the angel visited her almost two years earlier.

The baby grew still and listened quietly to her clear voice mingling with the soft Egyptian breeze: "My soul doth magnify the Lord, and my spirit hath rejoiced in God my Saviour . . ."

As she sang, a strange thing began to happen. A look of comprehension began to fill the baby's dark eyes. His expression became intent, and his tiny mouth smiled.

When the song was finished, the two of them sat silently, caught up in a unique design of love—a love of mother and son, both human and divine, temporal and eternal. Then Mary quickly leaned and kissed the boy. He laughed and returned her kiss with a hug. Swinging him onto her hip, she balanced the laundry with her free arm and stood. Slowly she started up the path to their village.

This year there would be no adoring shepherds or angel choirs; no blazing star would mark the passage of her son's first year. For now he was just another child, cherished just as any other. Her heart could not look beyond that now.

"Blessed birthday, Jesus," she whispered, and he clapped his chubby hands with glee.

Pamela Kennedy

Many Years Ago

The miracle of Christmas
Began many years ago
In a little town called Bethlehem
Beneath a star's bright glow.

Here the infant Jesus
Was born on Christmas Day,
And three wise men traveled far
To show they did believe.

From nearby hills the shepherds
   came,
Followed by their sheep.
Each bowed to greet the newborn
   King
As the town lay fast asleep.

Their hearts rejoiced, for each one
   knew
That he had been sent their way
To help and guide them, every one,
Forever and a day.

The true miracle of Christmas
Is hope and faith and love—
These gifts the Christ Child brought to
   all
From heaven high above.

LaVerne P. Larson

Witnesses

On that first Christmas night of old,
When stars were hanging low,
As shepherds watched their sheep
   at night
With campfires all aglow,

Appeared the angels suddenly
To sing of Jesus' birth;
They told the shepherds God's
   own Son
Had come that night to earth!

So the shepherds went to Bethlehem,
By holy messengers led,
And found our Savior nestled warm
In a humble manger bed.

They searched; they found;
   they witnessed;
And now around the earth
We celebrate the wonder
All find in Jesus' birth.

George L. Ehrman

There Were Shepherds

The shepherds heard the angels sing,
That night so long ago;
And suddenly a great light shone
And warmed them with its glow.

"Fear not, for unto you is born
In Bethlehem this day,
A Saviour, which is Christ the Lord,"
They heard the angels say.

"Oh, glory in the highest now!"
The heavens seemed to ring;
"Now go ye unto Bethlehem
And see this wondrous thing."

The shepherds left their quiet flocks
To seek the stable place
And marvel at the Holy Child,
The mother's radiant face.

They did not understand the things
They heard and saw that night;
They only knew that love had filled
Their hearts with hope and light.

Edith Shaw Butler

Where

There's a dear little church on top of a hill;
Though I've left it long since, I can see it there still.
It lingers in memory a thing of delight;

Its walls seem to echo once more "Silent Night."
I've wandered away from that beloved old church,
But wherever I go I continue to search.
How I wish now that I could so keenly see
Such things as were once, oh, so real to me!

Nothing but love and peace and goodwill
Could be found in that dear little church on the hill.
How I'd like to return, go back through the years
To that church on the hill and forget all my fears.
But time marches on; let me find here as there
Such peace, perfect peace.
Lord, this is my prayer.

Phyllis C. Michael

Photo Opposite
SOUTH WOODBURY, VERMONT
Gene Ahrens
H. Armstrong Roberts

A Child Again

With mistletoe and holly
And candles all aglow,
My heart is beating wildly;
I love this season so.

I hear the distant church bells
Ring out their old refrain,
And in my mind that moment
I am a child again.

I see myself at Grandma's
Quite early Christmas Day,
Surrounded by my presents
With balls and tinsel gay.

I see the Christmas table
With food and goodies piled,
So lovingly prepared by
That grandmother so mild.

I hear the Christmas carols,
The pumper organ plays,
And everyone is singing;
Those were the good old days.

And then when night was fallen
Grandpa a tale would tell—
The story of the Christmas Guest—
I still recall so well.

With mistletoe and holly
And candles all aglow,
I go back to my childhood—
Those days of long ago!

Georgia B. Adams

Memories

My heart goes home at
    Christmas;
I guess it always will—
Back to the childhood home I
    love,
The home once family-filled.

I see the presents wrapped and
    topped
With bows—gold, green, and
    red—
A book, perhaps a box of
    crayons,
A doll, and once a sled.

My heart goes home at
    Christmas;
I know it always will.
For with this joyous yuletide
My heart is memory-filled.

I hear the "Merry Christmas"
    sounds;
They echo loud and clear.
Still in my heart they are a part
Of this bright Christmas Year.

Loise Pinkerton Fritz

Painting Overleaf
AMERICAN HOMESTEAD WINTER
Currier & Ives, 1868

A Time for Remembering

Christmas is a time for dreaming
     of the Magi of long ago,
A time for remembering
     sleigh rides in the snow.

It's a time for singing carols
     beside a Christmas tree,
A time for lighting candles
     as if the world were free.

It's a time for giving presents
     to everyone we love,
A time for watching starlight
     in the heavens up above.

It's a time for hanging stockings
     with smiles on every face,
A time for making memories
     even time cannot erase.

It's a time for making snowmen
     by quiet country lanes,
A time for hanging ornaments,
     mistletoe, and candy canes.

And Christmas is a holy time
     we'll treasure through the years
As together we remember
     the laughter and the tears.

                    Clay Harrison

Holiday Delights

German Christmas Stollen

 ¾ cup milk, scalded
 ¼ cup sugar
 ½ teaspoon salt
 ¼ cup butter or margarine
 ¼ cup warm water (110 to 115°)
 1 package dry yeast
 2¾ cups unsifted flour
 ⅛ teaspoon ground cardamom
 ½ cup seedless raisins
 ¼ cup chopped citron
 ½ cup chopped pecans
 1 tablespoon butter or margarine, melted

To the scalded milk, add sugar, salt, and butter. Cool to lukewarm. Measure warm water into a large, warm bowl. Add yeast; stir until dissolved. Add lukewarm milk mixture, 2 cups of the flour and cardamom. Beat until smooth. Stir in remaining flour, raisins, citron, and pecans. Turn out on a lightly floured board and knead until smooth and elastic, about 5 minutes. Place in a greased bowl, turning to grease top. Cover. Let rise in a warm place until double in bulk, about 1 hour. Roll dough into an oblong shape about ½ inch thick. Brush with melted butter. Fold in half lengthwise. Place on a greased baking sheet; cover. Let rise in a warm place until double in bulk, about 45 minutes. Bake at 350° about 40 minutes. Ice with Confectioners' Sugar Frosting.

Confectioners' Sugar Frosting

 1 cup confectioners' sugar
 1 to 2 tablespoons hot milk or water

In a small bowl, add milk or water gradually to sugar. Blend until mixture is smooth; spread over stollen. Decorate stollen with candied cherries and nuts if desired.

Meltaway Maple Crisps

 ½ cup butter
 ¼ cup sugar
 1 teaspoon maple flavoring
 2 cups sifted cake flour
 ¾ cup chopped pecans

Cream butter; add sugar gradually. Add flavoring and beat until fluffy. Stir in flour and mix until a dough forms. Fold in pecans and press into a ball. Pinch off small pieces of dough and place on ungreased cookie sheet. Flatten cookies with glass dipped in sugar. Bake at 350° for 7 minutes.

Holly Wreath Pie

 2 envelopes unflavored gelatin
 ¼ cup sugar
 4 cups eggnog
 1 cup whipping cream, whipped
 ½ cup chopped maraschino cherries
 ½ cup chopped nuts
 1 baked pastry shell
   Green citron
   Red maraschino cherries

Combine gelatin and sugar in the top of a double boiler. Stir in 1 cup of the eggnog. Place over boiling water; stir until gelatin and sugar are dissolved. Remove from heat. Add remaining eggnog. Chill to consistency of unbeaten egg white. Whip until light and fluffy. Fold in the whipped cream, chopped cherries, and nuts. Turn into baked pie shell. Chill until firm. To decorate, make small holly wreaths of citron, cut into quarter-moon shapes and place on top of filling to form rings. Place a tiny piece of red maraschino cherry in the centers.

Christmas

The frost's on the window,
The wreath's on the door,
The Christmas tree's glittering
From ceiling to floor;

The candlelight flickers,
The firelight glows,
Stockings are hung neatly
All in a row;

The old folks, the young folks
Gather together,
From faraway places,
In all types of weather

To celebrate Christmas
And sing the refrain:
"Glory to God,
Peace on earth to all men."

Constance Quinby Mills

Home

December storms have painted all
The trees with frozen snow,
While outside on a Christmas Eve
The wintry winds do blow.

And though the paths are dark and long,
We travel through the night,
Just knowing in a little while
We'll meet a friendly light.

A child is fast asleep in back,
As quiet as a mouse,
Far off in dreams of what's in store
When we reach Grandma's house.

There Grandma jumps excitedly
At every distant sound,
And Grandpa sneaks a quick look, too;
None can settle down!

Oh, no pleasure could be sweeter
Or found another way
Than being all together
At home on Christmas Day!

Virginia Claire

Come Share the Christmas Fire

Come share the Christmas fire,
    Whose hearth is bright and glowing.
Lighted tapers flicker tiny spires
    And silhouette the snow a-blowing.

Come share a warming cup
    Where friends and family bide;
The joy of Christmas lifts spirits up
    With gaiety this Christmastide.

Come share the tinseled tree,
    The manger with its scented straw.
Sing of wise men, the nativity;
    Let rafters ring throughout the hall.

Come share the Christmas glory;
    Recount together once again
The ageless, wondrous story
    Of peace on earth, good will toward men.

Mildred L. Jarrell

Rachel's Little Star Tree

Five-year old Josh, my nephew, was speechless with excitement. He was to spend the weekend with us in the country, and he had been promised his very own Christmas tree. From our woods, he was to select a choice evergreen to take home to his parents and two-year-old sister, Rachel.

We trudged with a happy, observant little boy across the icy fields to the nearby woods. Not feeling the cold, Josh ran ahead, singing "Jingle Bells" with all his heart.

Our choices were abundant. We examined pine trees and cedar trees, tall trees and short trees, large trees and small trees. But at each one, Josh merely shook his head. After pointing out more than twenty evergreens, we had not found a single tree that he liked. We continued looking and urged Josh to choose one, but to no avail. None was good enough.

Now it was beginning to snow; and a cold, stinging wind whistled through the trees. It was time to make a choice and go home.

Finally, Josh pointed to a cedar tree that was barely five feet tall. "That's my tree," he stated.

We were puzzled by his selection; there were so many larger and more handsome trees around us. "Wouldn't you like a bigger one?" my husband asked.

"No, I'm sure this is just right," he replied firmly. "It's just right for Rachel."

"But this is your tree, not Rachel's," we reminded him.

"I have to keep my promise," he replied solemnly.

"What promise?" we both asked, surprised.

"You see," explained Josh, "I promised Rachel I'd find a tree that was just her size so she could stand in her high chair and put the star on top all by herself. That's what I promised her at home. That was our secret."

Watching the delighted child beside his tree, we felt his joy and warmth at unselfishly remembering another—the real spirit of the season. We shared his excitement as the small evergreen crackled with each stroke of the axe, and then fell.

Homeward bound at last, we sang a resounding last chorus of "Jingle Bells" as the sky darkened and we left the woods behind. We would always remember how a thoughtful five-year-old boy had reminded us of the real meaning of Christmas; and the tiny green tree we dragged behind us would always be remembered as "Rachel's Little Star Tree."

Elisabeth Weaver Winstead

Snowflakes

Out of the bosom of the Air,
    Out of the cloud-folds of her garments shaken,
Over the woodlands brown and bare,
    Over the harvest-fields forsaken,
      Silent and soft and slow
      Descends the snow.

Even as our cloudy fancies take
    Suddenly shape in some divine expression,
Even as the troubled heart doth make
    In the white countenance confession,
      The troubled sky reveals
      The grief it feels.

This is the poem of the air,
    Slowly in silent syllables recorded;
This is the secret of despair,
    Long in its cloudy bosom hoarded,
      Now whispered and revealed
      To wood and field.

Henry Wadsworth Longfellow

Country Chronicle

Come walk with me this sunny Christmas morning to a grove of pines. (My father called them watchtowers for the hawks and crows, turrets for the owls.) It is one of my favorite sanctuaries at any time of year. Its carpet of dried needles is the only luxurious rug I shall ever know, and its aroma exhilarates me. I stand to listen and the pines whisper to me in tender, wistful tones.

Here, last night's snow has blanketed forest and field and capped the reaching boughs of the stately evergreens. No wind stirs as we pass under a silent bower of white. The purity of this outdoor cathedral reflects the holiness of this season. As the artistry of nature unfolds before me, I know I am watching the handiwork of God, and my heart is filled with the splendor of creation.

Pines inspire me. They have felt the lash of winds, the burden of ice, the weight of snow; but they have endured. I gaze with awe into their spires, towering heavenward like the steeple on the old country church of my boyhood.

It is Christmas, when again I become a child of the hills who seeks the wonders of creation and the beauty of nature, who exults in the birth of our Savior. Here, I find joy and solace as I feel Christ's love for mankind and his message of love and everlasting peace.

As I peer into the treetops, I hear once more the psalmist's words: "I will lift up mine eyes unto the hills, from whence cometh my help."

Lansing Christman

December's Waltz

Winter orchestrates the dance
In chilling winds and biting air.
Snowflakes whirl and skip and prance,
Waltzing wildly without a care.

Bowing swiftly to their mates,
They turn and glide in perfect time.
Spinning on their magic skates,
Across the frozen fields they climb.

Lilting measures rise and fall
In time with flakes of white,
While all God's creatures watch the ball,
Bedazzled by the sight.

When gradually the music dies,
There's not a single sound
As small white dancers from the sky
Take rest upon the ground.

Ava M. Plover

WINTER ON THE FARM
Robert Sweet

The Woods in Winter

I took a walk through the woods today,
The snow was drifted and white.
The touch of winter magic there
Made such a thrilling sight.

Every treetop capped with snow,
Every bush a ball of white—
It was a sparkling fairyland
As pure and fresh as life.

Just as far as I could see
Was white and drifted snow,
From the hilltop up above me
To the valley down below.

Along the woodland trail I walked
That led to a frozen brook;
Cedar boughs beside me bent
To form a sheltered nook.

A deer I saw in the woods today
And a fox running jaunty and free,
And a crimson cardinal flashed my way
As it flitted from tree to tree.

I walked along the old rail fence
To where once a cabin stood,
Home of a pioneer family
Carved deep within the woods.

I seemed to be in a faraway land,
In a kingdom wondrously fair
With neither hustle nor hurry,
No signs of worry or care.

There was only the splendor that winter brings,
And everything seemed perfect and good.
My heart was filled with joy supreme
As I walked through the winter woods.

As I turned home with heart content,
I began to laugh and sing,
For I was filled with the magic
That only a woodland walk can bring.

Robin Brown

Velvet Shoes

Unnumbered snows have fallen from these skies
To bless the earth; yet there will always be
The same wide wonder and the glad surprise
Whenever housebound folk look out and see
The giant sheet spread out to cover all
The frozen ground, the sleeping grass, and flowers
Tucked down between the hills; and falling flakes
Can fascinate and entertain for hours.

Then, when the last pale wing is folded down,
A fairyland is there with trees of pearl
And crystal streams and diamond-studded roofs.
While down the roads, white velvet rugs unfurl.
Lean winter's cup is scant for beauty's thirst;
We greet each snow as though it were our first.

M. Kathleen Haley

A Winter Walk

We sleep, and at length awake to the still reality of a winter morning. The snow lies warm as cotton or down upon the windowsill; the broadened sash and frosted panes admit a dim and private light, which enhances the snug cheer within. The stillness of the morning is impressive. . . .

Silently we unlatch the door, letting the drift fall in, and step abroad to face the cutting air. Already the stars have lost some of their sparkle, and a dull, leaden mist skirts the horizon. A lurid brazen light in the east proclaims the approach of day, while the western landscape is dim and spectral still, and clothed in a sombre Tartarian light, like the shadowy realms. . . .

The sun at length rises through the distant woods, as if with the faint clashing swinging sound of cymbals, melting the air with his beams, and with such rapid steps the morning travels, that already his rays are gilding the distant western mountains. Meanwhile we step hastily along through the powdery snow, warmed by an inward heat, enjoying an Indian summer still, in the increased glow of thought and feeling. . . .

The wonderful purity of nature at this season is a most pleasing fact. Every decayed stump and moss-grown stone and rail, and the dead leaves of autumn, are concealed by a clean napkin of snow. In the bare fields and tinkling woods, see what virtue survives. In the coldest and bleakest places, the warmest charities still maintain a foothold. . . .

. . . Standing quite alone, far in the forest, while the wind is shaking down snow from the trees, and leaving only the human tracks behind us, we find our reflection of a richer variety than the life of cities. The chickadee and nuthatch are more inspiring society than statesmen and philosophers, and we shall return to these last as to more vulgar companions. In this lonely glen, with its brooks draining the slopes, its creased ice and crystals of all hues, where the spruces and hemlocks stand up on either side, and the rush and sere wild oats in the rivulet itself, our lives are more serene and worthy to contemplate. . . .

But now, while we have loitered, the clouds

have gathered again, and a few straggling snowflakes are beginning to descend. Faster and faster they fall, shutting out the distant objects from sight. The snow falls on every wood and field, and no crevice is forgotten; by the river and the pond, on the hill and in the valley. Quadrupeds are confined to their coverts and the birds sit upon their perches this peaceful hour. There is not so much sound as in fair weather, but silently and gradually every slope, and the gray walls and fences, and the polished ice, and the sere leaves, which were not buried before, are concealed, and the tracks of men and beasts are lost. With so little effort does nature reassert her rule and blot out the traces of men. . . .

Though winter is represented in the almanac as an old man, facing the wind and sleet, and drawing his cloak about him, we rather think of him as a merry woodchopper, and warm-blooded youth, as blithe as summer. The unexplored grandeur of the storm keeps up the spirits of the traveler. In winter we lead a more inward life. Our hearts are warm and cheery, like cottages under drifts, whose windows and doors are half concealed, but from whose chimneys the smoke cheerfully ascends. The imprisoning drifts increase the sense of comfort to sit over the hearth and see the sky through the chimney too, enjoying the quiet and serene life that may be had in a warm corner by the chimney side, or feeling our pulse by listening to the low of the cattle in the street, or the sound of the flail in distant barns all the long afternoon. No doubt a skillful physician could determine our health by observing how these simple and natural sounds affected us. We enjoy now, not an oriental, but a boreal leisure, around warm stoves and fireplaces, and watch the shadow of motes in the sunbeams. . . .

Now commences the long winter evening around the farmer's hearth, when the thoughts of the indwellers travel far abroad, and men are by nature and necessity charitable and liberal to all creatures. Now is the happy resistance to cold, when the farmer reaps his reward, and thinks of his preparedness for winter, and, through the glittering panes, sees with equanimity "the mansion of the northern bear," for now the storm is over.

Henry David Thoreau

Photo Overleaf
LAKESIDE IN WINTER
Larry Lefever
Grant Heilman Photography

Another New Year

Another new year—what shall I make
    of it?
    God gave it to me as a loan.
Shall I search for earth's cheer with its
    pretense and take it—
        Not bread for my soul but a
        stone?

Another new year—what shall I gather,
    Earth's tinsel, her glitter to show?
Another new year—what would I
    rather,
        A flash or a deep inner glow?

A year full of getting or a year full of
    giving
        The best that I have to give?
A year full of fretting or a year full of
    living
        The way that God wants me to
        live?

Another new year—what shall I make
    of it?
        God gave me the right to choose.
Another new year—God helping, I'll
    take it
        And give it to him to use.

                Phyllis C. Michael

New Year Wish

Perhaps a bit wiser,
A bit kinder, too,
A little bit braver,
A heart that's more true,
A touch of believing
I've not known before,
In joys I'm receiving
A little bit more.

A little more anxious
To reach out my hand,
Despite hurt or problems
To still understand,
Accepting the heartache
That life often brings,
A little more beauty
In life's simple things.

A prayer when I'm weary
As onward I trod,
A little more trusting,
Believing in God,
'Tis this I would wish for
Within moments dear,
Not a lot—just a little
This wondrous new year.

Garnett Ann Schultz

Merry Christmas from all of us at *ideals®*

ACKNOWLEDGMENTS

THE SEASON'S FIRST SNOWFLAKES from *A MONTH OF MONDAYS* by Mary Lou Carney, copyright © 1984 by Abingdon Press. Used by permission; AMERICAN HOMESTEAD WINTER illustration, entered according to Act of Congress in the year 1868 by Currier & Ives in the clerk's office of the District Court of the U.S. for the Southern District of New York; SANTA PASSES from *EDGAR A. GUEST BROADCASTING*, copyright 1935, The Reilly & Lee Co. Used by permission; CHRISTMAS CARDS by Edna Jaques from *THE GOLDEN ROAD,* copyright 1953 by Thomas Allen Limited. Used by permission of Thomas Allen & Son Limited, Ontario, CAN; ANOTHER NEW YEAR by Phyllis C. Michael, copyright 1968 in *SOURCEBOOK OF POETRY,* compiled by Al Bryant, published by Zondervan Publishing House. Used by permission of the author; THROUGH THE EYES OF A CHILD by Debbie W. Parvin, copyright 1982; THE CANDY CANE from *CHRISTMAS COULD-BE TALES (And Other Verses)* by Margaret Rorke, copyright 1984 by Northwood Institute Press, Midland, MI; A WINTER WALK taken from the *EXCURSIONS* volume of *THE WRITINGS OF THOREAU,* Riverside Edition, published by Houghton Mifflin and Company, 1893; SNOWFLAKES from *THE COMPLETE POETICAL WORKS OF HENRY WADSWORTH LONGFELLOW,* edited by H. E. Scudder, Houghton Mifflin, Boston, 1893. Our sincere thanks to the following whose addresses we were unable to locate: Virginia Claire for HOME FOR CHRISTMAS; Nancy L. Kratowicz for FRAGRANCE OF CHRISTMAS; Constance Quinby Mills for CHRISTMAS; Reverend Frederick H. Sterne for MAGNIFICAT from *THE MAGIC OF THE MANGER,* copyright © 1973 by Frederick H. Sterne, published by Dorrance and Company.